Can You Really Hear Me?

Overcoming Obstacles as an Hearing Impaired Individual

Leola Smith

ACKNOWLEDGEMENTS

I wish to personally thank the following people for their contributions- those that shared their knowledge and experiences and those who helped to create the book.

First and foremost I want to thank God for giving me a chance to grow.

My parents for believing and supporting me.

My grandmother and family for their leadership as hearing impaired individuals.

My oldest son G'Ivori Graham, whom is partially deaf, for his story has encouraged me to further tell my story.

My friend, Signae Mckiever for encouraging me to write my book. Without you I would not have made it this far.

Darriel Tanner for helping me to make this book become a success.

My cousins for sharing their stories of triumph and experiences of storms of life that we all go through as individuals.

Claudia Gordon and Curtis Pride, this has been a blessing having you be a part of my book. Thank you!

We all go through the storms of life, and we arise from it with great pride and strength, faith and good intention. Our challenges can produce great character if we follow our intuition.

DEDICATION

I want to dedicate this book to everyone with any special needs or person with any disabilities who is going through obstacles. I want to encourage you to never give up. You can do it! Now is time to turn can't into can. Whatever your dreams are, you can achieve them and become successful in life no matter what. You are your own person. Stay Audacious and Bold!!!

Table of Contents

Introduction

It was a clear and sunny day. Kimberly had been waiting for this morning all week. She had just graduated with a Bachelor's degree in Social Work and recently applied for a case manager position online. Last week, she got THE CALL for the interview.

She pulled out one of her favorite outfits and jumped in the car. Kimberly was on her way. Her future was looking brighter and brighter. As she headed to her destination, she started to think of the silly questions that were asked on the application like...Do you have any accommodations that are needed to assist you on this job? Can you hear, read, or write? The truth of the matter is Kimberly had lied on her application. The fact is Kimberly is hearing impaired. She'd faced discrimination before. In her experience, most people will disregard her without hesitating once it's apparent that she can't hear. She was excited about the opportunity. After all, they told her that they were impressed with her resume, and that she was definitely qualified, to say the least. Now all she had to do was get through the interview without an interpreter.

Kimberly pulled up to the building, and walked in with boldness and confidence. Fifteen minutes later, the secretary was escorting her to the office to start the interview.

"Kimberly Smith, nice to meet you," Ms. Carlson greeted her.

Kimberly did her best to read Ms. Carlson's lips.

"Nice to meet you, also," Kimberly replied.

"Please take a seat. Make yourself comfortable," said Ms. Carlson.

The interview started off great. Kimberly was doing a great job with reading Ms. Carlson's lips and was able to answer all the questions. Ms. Carlson was impressed until...

"Do you have a reliable phone by which you can be reached so that clients could reach you in case of an emergency?" Ms. Carlson asked.

"Yes, but it would be great if we could use text messaging," said Kimberly.

"Why is that?" Ms. Carlson asked.

"Because I am hearing impaired," said Kimberly.

Ms. Carlson looked startled. Suddenly, things didn't appear to be going as well as before.

"You don't look like it. You speak clearly like a hearing person, and you were able to answer all the questions," said Ms. Carlson.

"That's because I can speak English and read lips well," Kimberly replied.

"I'm curious. How would you be able to respond to a client on a home visit?" asked Ms. Carlson.

"I would communicate on a home visit just as I am with you now," said Kimberly.

"What if the client has her back towards you?" Ms. Carlson asked.

"Well I would have to prepare myself and make sure that client is aware that I am hearing impaired. And during conversations, no one should have their back towards anyone anyway," said Kimberly.

"I am not sure how that would work out. I am sorry, Kimberly, but we want to hire someone who can hear, and I am not 100% sure that you would be able to fulfill certain responsibilities," said Ms. Carlson.

Kimberly left the interview saddened and hurt. She really wanted the job. Unfortunately, there are so many others like Kimberly, and that is the reason I decided to write this book. The story is actually a true story. Kimberly is me.

When this happened to me the questions arose in my head, do they know the workforce law, to not discriminate against a person because of their disability? Do employers know that they are to provide accommodations for people with disabilities? What if I had not answered the questions in the interview correctly and honestly or explain my inability to communicate without reading lips, would I have even gotten the interview? In my heart, I didn't think it was fair to be denied because of my disability, but again, I had to put my faith in Gods ability to work it out. I never stopped believing, that someday, someone was going to hire me. This is some examples of the discrimination challenges we face with disabilities.

When we judge a person's worth, just remember it starts with treating all people as human beings. Every person has certain rights to pursuit happiness regardless of their disability. Why do people feel the need to sabotage, crush, hinder, belittle, avoid, and most of all unfairly reject people because they are a little bit different? I have learned not to let people determine my worth. If I just keep the faith and believe it is going to work out for my good. Every person has something good inside of them, therefore it's not a person's (disability) differences that gives others the right to determine your worth. No person with a disability should never internationally be made to feel bad, but just in case it happens, it's more to life than self- pity. Continue to focus on your strengths in order to defy the impossible and others ignorance.

Many times our disabilities require or demand more of us. We must continue to be overcomer by fighting back our fears. There is success, achievement, and accomplishments in every person, no matter what some might think of us. Set goals to overcome your obstacles and challenges by seeking until you find it. God has given every man a measure of faith, just continue to believe.

Being hearing impaired or having any other disability is not the only thing that can stop a person from becoming successful in life. There are other challenges as well. There could be a sickness, lack of finances, etc.

Confidence is KEY. It is more like your faith is being tested. We determine our limitation. How would it feel to take a walk in my shoes? It's simple. Treat people how you want to be treated. Respect people the way you want to be respected. Do not get offended when a hearing impaired or deaf individual repeat your conversation. They only repeat to make sure they have a better understanding of what is being said. For example, just because we dance to music doesn't mean we can hear the words. We feel the beat and follow along with the beat as if it were a firecracker or an explosion.

Hearing loss does not equal loss of intelligence. We can do the same thing others can do. Speaking for myself, I know that God brought me in this world for a reason. He placed me here, on this path, to show the world that anyone can achieve. My ancestors would be proud of the things I've accomplished in my life. I want my children and grandchildren to remember to never judge a book, by its cover. Get to know people. Give them a chance in life. Determination is what keeps me going.

There are five senses that we nourish and that is to hear, feel, see, touch, and smell. All of the senses enable us to adapt to this world. When there is a lack of one of those senses, the defense mechanism of the others kicks in. People protect themselves, their minds, and soul from the mean treatment of the world. The working senses become dominant to improvise from what other senses are lacking. The senses combine to give us some critical thoughts about what goes on around us, or give us a better understanding of the things that encompass us.

The purpose of this book is to help bring awareness to the mistreatment some people experience at the hands of others simply because they're considered "handicapped" or "disadvantaged". I want to bring awareness to all the deaf and partially deaf individuals all around the world. This will help us and others understand the value of what it is like to have this kind of social disability. It is also very important to become familiar with the laws and policies toward discrimination guidelines to protect ourselves in order to step up to certain degrees of consequences. We must know our rights and enforce the law when it comes to people trying to discourage and disregard us. We are not asking for your sympathy; we are asking for respect, a chance to be something in life, and the same privileges that others are receiving.

In fact, I am writing to prove that you can turn your lemons into lemonade… your nightmares into great dreams…your failures into victories…your tests in testimonies… your obstacles into steps to getting closer to your goals. You can go from victim to victor.

It was about 18 years ago when the infamous Chris Tucker coined, "Do You Understand the Words That Are Coming out of My Mouth?", from the hilarious, action packed movie *Rush Hour*. That has been the story of my life but with a flip side. I'm not Chris Tucker, but I kind of understood his frustration to say the least. As a hearing impaired individual, I would like to coin "Do You Understand the Words that Are **NOT** Coming out of My Mouth?"

> *"Life is not compassionate towards victims. The trick is not to see yourself as one.*
>
> *It's never too late! I know I've felt like the victim in various situations in my life, but it's never too late for me to realize that it's my responsibility to stand on victorious ground and know that whatever it is I'm experiencing or going through, those are just the clouds rolling by while I stand here on the top of this mountain! This mountain called Victory! The clouds will come, and the clouds will go. But the truth is that I'm high up here on this*

mountaintop that reaches into the sky! I am a victor. I didn't climb up the mountain. I was born on top of it!"

— <u>C. JoyBell C.</u>

Chapter 1

My Life

"I am not a victim. No matter what I have been through, I'm still here. I have a history of victory."

— <u>Steve Maraboli</u>, <u>Unapologetically You: Reflections on Life and the Human Experience</u>

I grew up in a two parent home. At first, I was the only sibling at that point in life with a hearing loss. Years later, my younger sibling became hearing impaired, also. It was the biggest challenge; I had to learn how to communicate with my parents and other siblings by reading their lips. My mother would take me to the speech therapist every other day so that I could improve my language and learn how to pronounce words the proper way. That helped me in the long run.

Growing up knowing that I was not the only one with hearing loss made things easier. I was aware that there were other members of my family like me. My grandmother, great-aunt, great-uncle, few of my aunts, uncles, and many of my cousins experienced hearing loss as well. One key component in my overall happiness was definitely family and childhood memories.

Around the age of 5 years old my parents learned that I had a hearing impairment. I was retained in 1st grade due to my inability to read on the same level as the other students.

I remember the days when my mom would let me ride the bus from school to visit my cousins, Thelma and Otis at their apartment complex called the Foster Height. Thelma and Otis were also deaf, but I loved going over their house from school every day. We could really relate to one another for obvious reasons, and sign language was our mode of communication. That is exactly how I learned to sign. Also, Otis was the best Dominoes player. Thelma and I would play games with him just about every day. He taught me well. During one of our times on the playground, my cousin, some friends, and I were talking about our favorite foods. Once I said that I loved spaghetti, everyone with the exception of my cousin, laughed at me. We couldn't understand why they were laughing. There was one boy in particular, who'd asked me to repeat myself only to mock and laugh at me again. It was then that I learned that I'd been pronouncing the word "spaghetti" wrong.

That's when my conscious hit me. I couldn't believe that he was laughing at that. My cousin and I ignored him and continued to play. Afterward, I would see him at school. He would always try to make fun of me in front of people. "Say spaghetti", he said. But I didn't care. I just ignored him. He probably still tells people stories about me to this day. But guess what? I'm winning. I'm still moving forward and overcoming the obstacles.

When I was a young girl, my Great Aunt Mildred used to babysit me. She taught me how to read lips and a little sign language. She is partially deaf. Aunt Mildred was so hilarious, and she said whatever came to her mind. I admired her for that. As I got older, I started going to daycare. When I was old enough to ride the bus, I would visit Aunt Mildred. She had four boys who were also hearing impaired. That was another piece of excitement because I never felt alone; I surrounded myself with others like me. My Great Uncle Sam, who lived two houses down from my Aunt Mildred, was deaf, too. So was his wife. Any Sunday or holiday we would spend time at my Grandma Gertrude's house (who is partially deaf) was a celebration. She is the leader of the family. She is a strong piece in our family puzzle. These are family traditions that still continue today.

I grew up in a Baptist Church while few of my family members went to a deaf church. My greatest fear was not being able to hear the words around me at my church. There were two things that I knew I was good at and that was lip reading and sign language. Even though my family could attend a deaf church, it wouldn't be fair because I was the only one with the hearing loss within my household. So I attended the regular church with them by choice. That was another learning experience for me. I learned how to overcome that obstacle. I found my way through it. Even though I couldn't hear or understand when my pastor preached the Word of God, I knew what I stood for and believed in. When I joined the church, I became an usher. I didn't join the choir because I didn't think that I had it in me due to my hearing loss. I thought people would laugh at me.

Well, a couple of years later, our church had State Conventional for the youth which is when we would travel to different churches throughout the region. We all went out of town for a week. A couple of members that I knew were already choir members and a few of us were ushers. We were informed by one of our chaperones that we will all have to sing in a group choir in front of thousands of people. I was afraid and worried about what others might say and think about me. I could have talked or cried my way out, but I didn't do any of that. My gut instinct kept leading me to give myself a chance to prove that I can do anything no matter what my circumstances were.

When that day came, I was nervous at first. However, it turned out pretty awesome. I started to get comfortable with myself, and I let my inner spirit guide me through the whole process. It felt so good to be able to hear myself and others shouting, singing, and praising. No one was looking at me. I was not the central focus. We all had a good time. There was so much shouting for joy in that choir. I overcame the obstacles that day. I am glad I followed my instincts instead of my thoughts of what others might have thought and felt. One thing I learned in life is that we all are human.

During my elementary years, I would attend classes like any other regular student. I mean why not? I was like any other student. I just needed special accommodations. That's it. My brain functioned properly. I had so much support at school, and there were a few resource teachers who really cared about helping students like me. I even had speech therapy at school. Both the teacher and speech therapist went above and beyond to make sure that their special students were getting the proper accommodation that they needed and deserved. Even if things had gone wrong, they were there to encourage us. They were the ones who protected us from obstacles. They acted as providers and protectors.

Although others would protect me, I still had to learn how to protect myself. I would always get yelled at and picked on by others, but that one person would continually go overboard. One day I decided that enough was enough. I knew that I wanted to be treated like a human being. What is the point of judging and belittling others? Well I took it upon myself and handled the situation by stepping up to that person. I took matters into my own hands. I had the opportunity to walk away from the outcome, but my inner conscience got the best of me that day.

I had some regrets about what I did, but at the same time it made me feel better about myself. Even if that person was wrong, violence is never the solution to solve a problem. I could have handled the situation a little bit more wisely. All that mattered was that I would be okay from then on out. That one person never bothered me again. We actually became friends afterwards. In life, an individual has to step up, protect, and guide herself in a good and positive way inside and out. I knew at that moment that even though I had my teachers, parents, and siblings to support me, they could not be there for me every second of the day.

During my pre-teen years, life really began for me. It was different from being in elementary school. There were all kinds of activities to get involved in such as sports, music, cheerleading, dance team, R.O.T.C., and more. During my first year of junior high, I knew this would be my chance to do what I wanted. I didn't have to think about my hearing loss or living out a family tradition. I knew that I could do whatever I put my mind to, and I could make my own decision. So my 7th grade year I got involved in all kinds of activities. I gave everything a chance. I was already a violin player. I tried basketball. I never in my life knew anything about it up until that point. So I was a bit nervous about not making the team due to my hearing loss and my lack of experience. I thought about not being able to hear my team roar, not knowing the plays the coach will call out, not being able to hear the referees blow their whistles, and not being able to hear the spirit of the crowd from the stands.

Eventually, I made the team because the coach was not the type of person who focused on my hearing loss at that time. All she cared about was if I knew how to follow rules and how to play basketball. I wasn't that good, and she knew it would take time for me to adjust. I was really excited to be a part of the team. One day when we had an away game, I made the biggest mistake in my life. When our team was playing against the other team, I got a rebound. I mean I was so excited that I had the ball in my hand that I shot it in the hoop. The next thing I noticed was that I made the shot in the wrong hoop. I didn't hear my teammates calling my name to stop me from going the wrong way. I felt so embarrassed. I thought that my team mates were upset with me, but they weren't. They forgave me. This gave me comfort.

I was also a part of the track team. I didn't have any problems on the track. I was pretty fast out there. I had some challenges in middle school, but I enjoyed the experience and the path that it led me to.

During my high school years, I overcame some fears and challenges. I did feel a little down because I wasn't considered 'normal', but I learned in life that no one is perfect or better than the next person. There is more to life than having a hearing loss. Now that I am an adult, I have matured and grown a lot. I defeat obstacles a lot quicker these days.

Life after college

I finally earned my Bachelor's and Master's degrees. I thought that earning my degrees would help me to get a job easier despite my hearing loss. Well turns out, having a degree didn't really matter. I had been on about ten to fifteen interviews without an interpreter because people didn't want to hire an interpreter for me. Logical thought. But it is best to have a witness with you during interviews. You never know what might happen behind closed doors. People can say very rude things, and they have no idea that they are breaking the law.

Out of all of the interviews I attended, I received one job offer. A few of years later, I was offered a job as a Program Director for 3 years in home healthcare services. This brought me joy because they didn't see me as my 'disability'. They gave me a chance because I went to school for it and deserved to grow and learn more in my field. I am glad to have experienced that growth.

Chapter 2

Not A Victim

Do not assume an individual who has ears, can hear!!!

-Leola Smith

As the middle aged audience of music lovers eagerly waited for the concert to begin, they started conversing with one another. Words and phrases such as "genius", "greatest of all time", "heavenly music", and "extraordinary" echoed throughout the sold out legendary hall. Suddenly the curtains opened, and the crowd applauded.

First came the stroke of the piano keys. Then came the strings of the violins and cello. And suddenly, all the instruments in unity began to create a perfect melody. Pure art hit the stage. For two hours, the audience was awed by the intriguing sounds of the symphony. At the last stroke of the piano, the audience stood on their feet and began to clap, for they had enjoyed themselves. Who was the composer of this mesmerizing music? Who so brilliantly produced the symphony? As shocking as this may seem, this music came from a deaf man by the name of Beethoven. Beethoven spent the latter end of his life as hearing impaired, yet he still went on to compose six symphonies, four solo concerti, five string quartets, six string sonatas, five sets of piano variations, four overtures, four trios, two sextets, and seventy-two songs… without hearing.

HE OVERCAME

In 1916, during World War I, in Carnegie Hall, these words were uttered from an extremely remarkable woman:

To begin with, I have a word to say to my good friends, the editors, and others who are moved to pity me. Some people are grieved because they imagine I am in the hands of unscrupulous persons who lead me astray and persuade me to espouse unpopular causes and make me the mouthpiece of their propaganda. Now, let it be understood once and for all that I do not want their pity; I would not change places with one of them. I know what I am talking about. My sources of information are as good and reliable as that of anybody else. I have papers and magazines from England, France, Germany and Austria that I can read myself. Not all the editors I have met can do that. Quite a number of them have to take their French and German second hand. No, I will not disparage the editors. They are an overworked, misunderstood class. Let them remember, though, that if I cannot see the fire at the end of their cigarettes, neither can they thread a needle in the dark. All I ask, gentlemen, is a fair field and no favor. I have entered the fight against preparedness and against the economic system under which we live. It is to be a fight to the finish, and I ask no quarter.

She was a very powerful woman… an eloquent speaker… humanitarian…leader… author…activist…She was simply an overcomer. Those were some of the words from one of the ninety two speeches she had given. She was the author of twelve books, was awarded the Presidential Medal of Freedom, and was the first woman to graduate with an honorary degree from Harvard... just to name a few. Ms. Helen Keller was both blind and deaf.

SHE OVERCAME

There in a research lab in West Orange, New Jersey, stood a man who had spent countless days working on the possibility of creating a world changing invention. He couldn't help but to think about the future and how this particular product would change the way the world would be entertained and possibly educated. It would be more than just reading a book and capturing a moment through a still picture...eventually maybe the book could turn into a film and the picture into a video. After much research and hard work and thinking, the motion picture camera was produced, and the inventor Thomas Edison had done it again. Despite his hearing loss, Edison invented the first light bulb, fluoroscope, rechargeable battery, telephone transmitter, and more and holds 1,093 US patents.

HE OVERCAME

The FBI agents sat around the table anxious to find out if they had finally discovered the video tape that would put an end to a 3 year drug ring. Detective Watson walks into the office with the video tape in his hand. They had been working extremely hard to solve this case. Detective Watson plays the tape only to find out that the image is blurry, and there was no sound. The agents all looked at each other in disappointment, but Detective Watson urged them all to keep hope alive because he knew of someone who may be able to help. He then walks outside to make a phone call. Forty five minutes later, in walks Detective Watson with a woman by the name of Sue, Sue Thomas that is.

Sue Thomas was the first deaf person to work for the FBI as a lip reader to help them solve cases. She was very essential in helping them to catch the criminals and keep the environment as safe as possible. She worked with the FBI for 3-4 years. Thomas landed her own TV series called *Sue Thomas: F B Eye* which was a television show that depicted her life in working with the FBI. The show had over 3 million viewers.

SHE OVERCAME

There are other Beethovens, Edisons, Thomases, and Kellers in the world. We were all created for greatness, but if we don't understand how to overcome, we will never see the victories and accomplishments that Beethoven witnessed. Everyone goes through obstacles at different points in their lives. I want to accomplish EVERYTHING in life. Life was created to be conquered and fulfilled.

Since I have now found ways to communicate with other people besides text messages, I do not have to rely on anyone to do anything for me. I am my own person. I can set goals where I tell myself how far in life I can go. No one can determine that but me. My intention leads me to better things.

Also, I am still in search for a job, but I have now been operating in my purpose. I do things that can make my life successful by telling my story, building my brand, and starting a business with a great friend. I want my kids to grow up knowing that their mother worked hard for them.

I want them to know that no matter what negative situation I encountered, I conquered it. Sometimes in life I want give up because people gave up on me. But I'm stronger than that. My faith and intentions are stronger.

I OVERCAME

Chapter 3

Don't Believe The Hype

According to the Hearing Loss Association of America:

"About twenty percent of Americans, forty eight million, report some degree of hearing loss. At age sixty five, one out of three people has a hearing loss. Sixty percent of the people with hearing loss are either in the work force or in educational settings. While people in the workplace with the mildest hearing losses show little or no drop in income compared to their normal hearing peers, as the hearing loss increases, so does the reduction in compensation. About two to three of every one thousand children are hard of hearing or deaf. It's estimated that thirty school children per one thousand have a hearing loss."

With those alarming numbers, society should seek to understand and act upon truth. I believe that most people that discriminate are just ignorant of reality and really don't understand what hearing impairment really is. They don't understand the challenges we face and the adjustments that have to be made.

When I am around people who don't know me and my situation and am conversing with them, they have a strange look on their face. They normally tell me that I have an accent, and they go on to ask me where I'm from. I tell them that I'm from another world. One day I was out of town with my family. We were at this hotel. It was around morning time. I stopped to ask this guy if they had any more banana nut muffins, which was my favorite. He asked me to repeat myself, and I did. After that he asked me where was I from and why did I talk like 'that'. Then he invited his coworker over to come hear me talk. I was trying my best to hold it together and not laugh. He didn't know my situation and neither did the coworker. He just wanted to hear my voice. My Aunt Ann heard him and she stepped up and informed him that I was hearing impaired. He backed off and apologized. I forgave him and moved on.

It is very important to not believe the hype. You must discover the truth for yourself. There are a few misconceptions about those who have hearing loss, and ignorance leads to those misconceptions. Sometimes people have the wrong information and tend to judge a book by its cover. I don't judge people based on their ignorance. I just simply supply them with the accurate information. For example, there are two technological devices that have been great towards the breakthrough in advancement for those with hearing loss.

One misconception is that sometimes people think that a hearing impaired person is faking their hearing loss just because they can't give them feedback so quick when they communicate. No, that is not true! We are trained well to learn how to communicate by reading lips. All that screaming, hollering, and loud talking at us is not going get you anywhere and leads to a reiteration of communication. Just stop and save your energy! Keep your tone of voice moderate. We have loss of hearing which can be mild or moderate. So we talk loud to hear ourselves, but sometimes we talk soft.

Another misconception is that we can hear extremely well with hearing aids. That is not necessarily true. When it comes to communicating with other people, it's all about the way they carry their speech, how their lips shape, and the clarity of the words flowing out of their mouths. For those who are not good lip readers, they use sign language to adapt. Therefore, we are raised and taught to know certain vocabulary by reading lips or by sign language. So vocabulary is our struggle.

Our way of understanding nonverbal communication falls in the category of body language. That is how some of us observe an individual. We are trying to understand them and examine them in a way that helps make it easier to read them. Give us a chance to send and receive the message. This body language puts a hearing impaired individual in a safe place which leads to effective communication. One must simply seek to understand a situation for what it really is before making a conclusion.

The most known misconception is that people who have a hearing loss are unintelligent or slow. Well, I beg to differ. I am a living witness, having legitimately earned a college degree and having become a well-educated woman.

The Alexander Graham Bell Association article, "Dispelling Myths about Deafness" states, "Recent studies show that children who solely utilize listening and spoken language, rather than a combination of this with ASL, demonstrate better listening and spoken language skills than do children who follow a combination approach, and that these children frequently develop expressive and receptive language test scores similar to their typical hearing peers. The voices of our deaf children tell the story. In videos available on AG Bell's YouTube channel, families share the remarkable abilities of deaf children today—making music, singing songs, and participating fully in sports, theater and more with wonderful speech and remarkable hearing.

"What it means to be "deaf" has changed. Deaf children growing up today have unprecedented opportunities to develop listening and spoken language, thanks to newborn screening, early identification and intervention, and the latest technology, such as advanced hearing aids and cochlear implants."

The majority of hearing impairment individuals adjust in this world by using a specialized device called a hearing aid which amplifies the sounds that surround them. There is another device called a **cochlear implant**. Unlike the hearing aids, this device substitutes the function of the damage in the internal ear. Hearing aids and cochlear implants are miraculous and such a blessing. They give us another chance to hear those sounds of different voices. They are EPIC! Even when a person that has a hearing loss has their back turned, they can still hear the words you say. Communication still needs to be face to face or involving eye contact at all times no matter what.

We also adapt through technology. There are devices like cell phones, IPads, Tango, Face-Time, and social media connections that give others an opportunity to communicate easier. Most times, when we want to call family, friends, etc., we use services called Relay Services.

It's a two-way communication tool that connects us through devices known as TTY's, VCO, and Sorenson. These three tools allow us a unique privilege to communicate effectively with one another. When we go to places like the bank, store or the doctor's office and find that there is no interpreter, we have to inform them. We need to inform them of the hearing impairment and that we need to communicate in a particular way. Most of the time, communication can be written back and forth on paper. Television shows, movies, DVDs, and YouTube videos provide captions in which the words flow across the bottom of the screen.

Other devices alert hearing impaired individuals such as the doorbell. When it rings, a light flashes which signals that someone is at the door. Even when the phone rings it sends a sensor to the light to flash. Most importantly, when an individual has an infant or toddler, there are devices like the Sonic Sitter that informs the parents when the baby cries or moves. There are also medical alerts. These devices allow us to be independent and free. We don't have to depend on others so much.

Another way of adapting in this world is earning a college degree which is an enormous challenge when it comes to job seeking. Education plays a key role in your success and opens many doors. People will always test our assumption, but you still must press past that to reach your goals. You don't have to have a victim's mentality when you have a "disability". There are a lot of tools now-a-days to assist us with our communication and language development.

Now that I have provided a little enlightenment, I hope you will gain a better understanding of the life of those who experience hearing loss. I will not only share my story, but I will share the story of successful others also. Remember this is not just for hearing impaired individuals, but it is for anyone who has been offended or frowned upon because of their skin color, height, weight, gender, their inability to see, lack of reading skills, etc.

Chapter 4

Defying All Odds

We can accomplish goals in spite of our limitations, no matter what kind of disability or challenge we have.

-Claudia Gordon

People who have hearing loss should not be exempt from society. We have goals and dreams also. Contrary to popular belief, we are just as in tuned to the world as those who have not experienced hearing loss. I love my cousin Meka's definition of success. She describes success as being able to reach your goals and being a role model to your children. Although she at one point has felt left out as a hearing impaired individual, she puts God first in everything. That will lead her in the right direction.

GORDON NUGGETS from Former Senior Policy Advisor for Homeland Security and current White House Liaison to the disability community.

I had a phenomenal opportunity to interview Claudia Gordon on her thoughts towards the theme of this book.

From Jamaica to the White House, Claudia Gordon has obtained tremendous success despite all odds. At the age of eight, Gordon woke up one morning and could no longer hear. She had become deaf overnight, but she did not allow that to prevent her from fulfilling her dreams and excelling at everything she puts her hands to. Growing up deaf wasn't easy for her, but today her name is prevalent throughout the nation. In reference to discrimination among the deaf population, Gordon was very adamant in her stance for equality. She stated, "The attitude towards what people can or cannot do is a major factor, and communication is what binds people together. Attitude affects how people communicate with one another. Discrimination brings about isolation and when there's a communication gap, there could be a level of discomfort in not wanting to say the wrong thing."

She went on to explain that there should be reasonable accommodations for the deaf… opportunities to get the desired job, proper resources based upon whether an employee would thrive on the job, staff meetings having interpreters… ACCESSIBILITY…

For Gordon it was a constant struggle as a young girl and teen. Even as a college student she had challenges, but she didn't expect anything less of herself. She graduated with Honors from Howard University and Washington College of Law making her the first deaf African American female lawyer in the United States. **OUTSTANDING**.

She never settled and continued to fight through the discrimination and lack of accommodations. Gordon took the road less travelled, and it made all the difference. Challenging herself and small victories have been key elements to her success.

Before the interview ended Gordon shared a **FEW GORDON NUGGETS**.

1. Choose to be smart over being popular.

   She invested her time in improving her life. "Be comfortable with being alone," she said. She read a lot of books. "Education is powerful and a great tool for achieving the impossible," she stated.

2. **Have a real strong sense of belief**.

   The only person that can stop you is you. You have to believe in yourself. There will be voices of doubt. People can continue to doubt, but you have to continue to strive to make your dreams happen. "My life is what I make it," said Gordon. Never become a victim. Work hard and persevere.

3. **Be uniquely you**.

   No one can make you inferior without your consent. Gordon embraced every aspect of her life. Womanhood... Black Community...Deaf Community...Law and Government Industry. Gordon gives her time, talent, and resources to each one of those facets of her life. She didn't deny who she was. After all, that is what makes her "UNIQUELY HER".

Coach Pride Shares Tid-Bits of His Experience and Success

I also had an opportunity to interview Curtis Pride.

In the 90s, Curtis Pride made history in becoming the first deaf full season Major League Baseball player. He is currently the head baseball coach at Gallaudet University. Pride has had major success, but had to defy all odds as well. He states that there are advantages and disadvantages to being deaf. Although he wasn't able to hear music, hear on the phone, or be involved in group conversations, he learned to be keenly alert of his surroundings, focus on tasks, and read lips at a distance. Also while playing on the baseball field, he was unable to hear the "boos" and negative comments from the opposing fans. In other words, he wasn't distracted from the outside noises. He describes one of his defining moments as being when he made his first major league hit, a pinch hit a two run double that sparked the Expos (his team) comeback to beat the Phillies during the pennant race in 1993. That hit resulted in an emotional five minute standing ovation which lasted through the entire pitching change. Pride ascribes his success to a strong support system made up of his parents, sisters, childhood friends, classmates, teachers, and coaches. Strong self-belief, determination, and goal orientation also played a huge role in his success.

Both Gordon and Pride are overcomers and have obtained successful lives that are admirable to others, especially me. It is great to hear from individuals you can relate to. If they can do it, so can you. What I've learned from having the grand opportunity of interviewing them both is that all things are possible regardless of any "handicaps". Defying all odds is the matter of confidence, diligence, and mental strength. I not only took out the time to interview people who have made history, but I also had a great opportunity to interview everyday people who have hearing loss. We all may just be able to relate to these answers.

Question: What is the hardest part about being hearing impaired?

Cristi: At times, growing up as a hearing impaired student felt like being in a bottomless pit of confusion. It is not always bad because I had already learned to accept myself for who I was. It was sometimes a struggle if I couldn't see notes that were up on the board while the teacher was talking. I would have to wait until the teacher would finish her notes so I can see and write it down, but all the other students would finish ahead of time. Sometimes they would have to wait on me to finish copying the notes so the teacher would continue. As I got older, in high school, I managed to write down the notes faster so the other students wouldn't have to wait. I had a best friend who was also deaf throughout elementary to high school, and we were always placed together in the same class, right next to each other. Therefore, it was easier for me because I had someone to talk to that could relate to me. I have learned to cope with the frustrations of being hearing impaired, but I never had a problem making friends. There are advantages to being hearing impaired. I can turn off my hearing aids so if there are loud noises that bother me or people arguing or kids being loud (especially when I go to bed without my hearing aids) I can sleep well. Being hearing impaired in the real world is difficult because of the job force and some of the actions of people who are ignorant towards the lifestyle of those who are deaf. But I have learned to make the best of it and work harder for something I want.

Question: What is your definition of success?

Cristi: My definition of success is to not let anyone tell me anything different or pessimistic about my hearing impairment and to believe in myself. I succeeded in trying out for the band in 6th grade and made it when they told me I wouldn't be able to hear all the sounds. All I had to do was read the music notes and follow the beats. I succeeded in trying out for the dance team in 6th grade, junior high, and throughout high school. I learned to overcome my obstacles and face challenges and things came my way.

Question: What are your major accomplishments?

Cristi: My major accomplishment was getting a high school diploma and having experienced working at big companies to see the good, the bad, and the ugly and opportunities to acquire diplomacy and political skills. Right now, my biggest goal is to finish college.

Question: What are major life lessons that you have learned?

Cristi: My major life lesson that I've learned is to never let anyone take advantage of or underestimate me because of my hearing impairment and to speak up for my rights and have patience.

The second interview was a pleasure as I interviewed my cousin Terrence ...capturing moments from the next generation.

Question: What is the hardest part about being hearing impaired?

Terrence: The hardest part is proving that you can do something. For example, when I play football, the coaches would think that my 'hard of hearing' would be a bad thing. So I have to prove myself and work harder than anybody on and off the field.

Question: What is your definition of success?

Terrence: Success to me is providing for your family and helping them as well as setting an example for the younger generation.

Question: What are your major accomplishments?

Terrence: Getting all A's. Getting put in a newspaper.

Question: What are major life lessons that you have learned?

Terrence: Everything is not going to come to me. I have to work hard for it, and I learned that you can't trust everybody.

These interviews were notes from the wise and experienced. Listening to these interviews inspire me to keep pressing and to know that I am not alone. There are people who do not and will not allow circumstances to keep them from pursuing success as they would have it.

Chapter 5

Life Lessons

In my life, I've lived, I've loved, I've lost, I've missed, I've hurt, I've trusted, I've made mistakes, but most of all I've learned.

-Unknown

Everyone has a story, and weaved inside of those stories are life lessons. Some stories are more dramatic than others, but in every story there is a treasure… a treasure by which if explained well could right the wrongs in your life and in the lives of others. In this chapter, I have included 7 life lessons that I have learned and applied throughout my journey.

Lesson 1: Never Stop Believing in Yourself

Always believe in yourself. No matter who's around you being negative or thrusting negative energy at you, totally block it off because whatever you believe, you become.

Michael Jackson

One of the most powerful forces on earth is belief. Men and women have defied nature based upon what they believed in. Believing in oneself is necessary. You can just about read or listen to any interview of an accomplished individual and discover that one of his or her traits is confidence. They had to believe in themselves first. It is impossible to win at life if you don't do so. I'm pretty sure Muhammed Ali had confidence in himself before he became a boxing champion. I'm pretty sure Oprah Winfrey first believed that she could be the number one television show host in the world. I've had to believe in myself to accomplish what I was once afraid of and incapable of doing. People think that just because they experience limitations and "handicaps" that they can't achieve certain things. I beg to differ.

I want something more out of life. So, I attended Grambling State University and earned a BA degree in Social Work. The reason why I choose that field was because it is inspiring, and it is my passion to help others. I am able to give back to others to make them aware that they are not alone out there. Also, I went back to get my Master's Degree from the University of Phoenix in Psychology. I love to observe and study different mindsets and behaviors. Both these degrees opened doors for me to have the opportunity to go out and show others that we can do this. You just have to find your niche and go for it. That is what I did.

I wouldn't have gotten both a bachelor's and master's degree if I didn't believe in myself. I saw myself accomplishing big goals, and I still do today. Through the opposition and hindrances, I definitely realized that I couldn't accomplish anything if I didn't think that I could. I believed it; therefore, I acted on it.

Lesson 2: Forgive the Ignorance

Weak people revenge. Strong people forgive. Intelligent people ignore.

-Anonymous

Unfortunately, there will always be ignorance in this world. I, for one, have experienced a lot of it. When you understand the true definition of the word, it'll be easier to forgive.

Merriam Webster Dictionary defines ignorance as "a lack of knowledge, understanding, or education." People act out of ignorance because they simply are misinformed or uninformed. People's ignorance can hurt your feelings, upset you, intimidate you, and perhaps embarrass you.

Cynthia was so excited about this new adventure. Finally, she would be on her own to experience the joys of college. Freedom. Life. Responsibility. Education. So many great things. Right? So one may think.

One day Cynthia's cousin Carla called her up. She wanted to visit her cousin on this beautiful campus to get a feel of what college life was all about. They visited one of the resource advisors. What happened next stunned the both of them. As Cynthia was speaking with the advisor, she found herself not really understanding what the advisor was saying. The advisor then asked, "WHY DON'T YOU HAVE ON YOUR HEARING AIDS?" Cynthia explained that her battery was dead.

"Your hearing loss is your problem, not mine," the advisor rudely stated.

Both Cynthia and her cousin were able to read her lips word for word. At that moment, so many thoughts ran through Cynthia's head. *What do you mean 'this is not your problem? I never said that it was your problem. Wait, aren't you here to help? Isn't that what you get paid to do? Is this an act of discrimination? Is she taking advantage of my "problem? I don't believe I have a problem. I should report her.*

However, both Cynthia and her cousin were able to calm themselves down and respond in a mature fashion about the situation. But how crazy is that? They were shocked and appalled. Or shall I say my cousin and I were shocked and appalled because Cynthia's story is my story.

My sister tells this story:

I remember looking for an apartment with a friend a year after high school. I had a good job and was working at Chase. I made decent money to get an apartment, and it was my first job. What I didn't know in the real world was that there was and still is going to be discrimination because of my hearing impairment. I found one apartment I loved, and it was a townhouse. I had talked with the landlord to find out the rental cost and leasing information. The landlord gave me information and said to call for availabilities.

I was confused because we had saw some apartments that were empty by peeking in to see what the inside looked like before we went to the office to talk with the landlord. Why would he tell me to call when we could clearly see that there were some available. I had my friend to call and check the availabilities while I was at work. After work, I asked my friend what the landlord said, and he told me not to worry about this one and to continue to look for other apartments. I told him that I wasn't going to do that and that I wanted to know what the landlord said. He didn't really want to tell me because he knew it was going to hurt my feelings. I forced the answers out of him. He said that the landlord wasn't going to give me the apartment because I was deaf.

That was a great example of ignorance. You can choose to dwell on it or move forward. Inequality has always been around. When you are hearing impaired, people tend to treat you as if you are an inconvenience. Whatever rationalization the landlord had in his head didn't lead to an informed decision. It was solely based on ignorance.

Forgiveness is vital in a continuation of one's journey. Holding on to anger and bitterness is a dead weight that deters many people from fulfilling their potential. Forgiving someone that wronged you is not easy, but it is necessary. You can't spend years being bitter and expect to move forward, at least not at a reasonable pace. If I had never forgiven all the ignorant people I encountered, I wouldn't be writing this book. Besides, you are only hurting yourself when you don't forgive.

Lesson 3: Recognize Those Who Have Your Best Interest at Heart

Although I have experienced discrimination and ignorance, I still had supportive people in my corner. Sometimes when you get upset and bitter about your situation or experience mistreatment, you tend to not recognize those who have your best interest at heart. God has placed some wonderful people in my life and on my path. My family has been very supportive. My parents did everything that they could to help me discover and live up to my God-given potential. They were vigilant in making sure that I received fair and equal treatment. If anyone had my back, it was my parents. My parents didn't just recognize discriminative behavior, they confronted it. They believed in protecting my rights, and for that I'm grateful.

Then there were my teachers. I encountered several teachers and speech therapy staff members who made a difference in my life and went above and beyond in making sure I had the proper accommodations. When things went wrong, they were there to encourage me. I remember Mrs. Schween, she was one of my elementary school teachers. She used to take me to her house to have ice cream or just play with her kids. In middle school there was Mrs. Nickolas. She was an amazing school resources teacher. In high school, there were Mrs. Clark and Mrs. Hines. They helped guide me through my high school years.

Don't be so over powered with negativity that you aren't able to focus on the blessings that surround you daily.

Lesson 4: Setting Goals

Give me a stock clerk with a goal, and I'll give you a man who will make history. Give me a man with no goals, and I'll give you a stock clerk.

-J.C. Penney

Setting goals is a prerequisite for achieving success. Goal setting is very important. Goals are defined as a target or plan of a desired outcome. Most successful people attribute their success to their habit of writing down their goals. It's something about writing them down and taking action. One of the top business coaches in America, Dr. Stacia Pierce says, "What is written is real."

Before most contractors begin laying the foundation for a building, they have what you call a blueprint. It would be awfully hard to build something without one. A blueprint is simply a plan, sketch, or layout of the design. Your goals represent the blueprint for your life. People just don't all of a sudden wake up and say I want to be famous, and it just happens. Life doesn't work that way. Setting goals and acting on them are what create real success. The ones who normally lose the weight, get the promotion, become millionaires, pay off their debts, make the team, or win the competition are the ones who wrote down their goals with the intention to actually execute.

I'm pretty sure Booker T. Washington set goals to start a very wealthy and successful school during slavery times and rise from humble beginnings to fame... or that Mark Victor Hansen and Jack Canfield set goals to become renowned authors selling five hundred million copies of Chicken Soup for the Soul... or that Dr. Seuss set goals to become one of the world's top children book authors in writing sixty books... or that, let's make it more relatable... or the magna cum laude set goals to maintain a 4.0 through the entire college career... or that freshmen set goals to make the varsity squad...or the new CEO of the company set goals to climb up the ladder of success.

I remember as a kid getting involved with different activities. I set out goals despite my hearing loss. I would give it a chance. I set a goal to learn the violin, so I did. I set a goal to make the basketball team, so I did. I set a goal to make the track team, so I did. I set a goal to earn two degrees, so I did. Anytime I want to achieve something, I set it as a goal first and go for it. Developing the habit of goal setting has changed my life and put me on the path to success.

Lesson 5: Treat Others the Way You Want to Be Treated

So in everything, do to others what you would have them do to you.

Matthew 7:12

The Golden Rule teaches us to treat others the way we want to be treated. As a person who has faced discrimination, I know how it feels to be mistreated. I for one wouldn't wish that feeling upon anyone. The way you treat others tells a lot about you. What goes around comes around. You actually do reap what you sow. I've learned to respect others because you never know who you're in the midst of. Life can sometimes be like a boomerang. I am glad I learned this lesson throughout my journey.

One story goes:

A lady was left by her husband to raise 4 kids on her own. Within 4 months of her husband's departure, she fell into depression because she felt that she couldn't raise 4 kids on her own. She had a decent job but not enough to sustain the necessities of 4 children, plus the house and car.

Her car was repossessed, and she was three months behind on rent. She got the idea to apply for a short term loan to help her catch up with the bills and get back on track as she was going out for the new promotion at her job. She tried several banks but was denied. She went home and found the mail on the kitchen table. As she was going through the mail, she opened one of the envelopes and discovered that there was a $5000.00 check. She began to cry in excitement and shock. A letter that came with the check read:

Dear Karen,

I was thankful that God heard my prayers... five years ago when you allowed my daughter to live with you and your family for a year for free while I was going through a drug rehabilitation program, I prayed and asked God to help me to one day be able to be a blessing to you as you had been to my daughter and me. I thought everything was crazy because you had only met me once, and I was like a stranger. However because you were a mother also and could relate, you decided to step in. Well God answered my prayers which was why I sent you this check. I know after I left the program, I moved back to Chicago and we lost contact with one another. I've been doing well. I now own one of the top cleaning businesses in my area, and Angela will be going to high school in the fall. She is a straight A student. Thanks again for helping out a stranger. Please stay in contact.

Love,

Sharon

Stories like these warm my heart, but there is a flip side as well.

One man tells a story that he regrets. Mr. Brent was known as a tough high school teacher. He had one student by the name of Terry who always had an excuse for not turning in work because he and his family were experiencing hardship. When Terry didn't show up for the final exam, he failed him. Terry showed up later that week to make up the exam, but he didn't allow him to take the test. In this particular school district, make up work opportunities are left up to the teachers regarding if the student would be allowed to make up the exam. Fast forward five months later... Mr. Brent's wife had begun to get sick. Their college aged son had been travelling back and forth to visit his mother, and he had missing work. He wanted to be by his mother side and missed the final exam. When he went to take the test, his professor wouldn't allow him to make it up.

Sounds familiar? Your character does not only affect you, but it could affect your children also. That's why it is important to treat others fairly. You never know what could happen. It could work against you or for you.

Lesson 6: Don't Forget Them That Are Less Fortunate

I also learned to be a giver and to be generous towards others, especially those who are less fortunate. Being a blessing to others leads to more happiness in your life. In all of my success and failures, I've always had the less fortunate in mind because I understand the importance of helping those who may be unable to help themselves.

Lesson 7: Never Give Up

I've learned in life to never give up. Have hope and faith. The sky is the limit. You might not get what you want now, but it will eventually come to you on time. Always know what your expectation is in life. Set goals and vision board your life and let your intentions lead you to the right path. Believe me, there will be some struggles, setbacks, and obstacles along that journey. However, it will be a great adventure and life story to tell. Figure out what you want out of life and determine where you're going. Quitters never accomplish anything. I wouldn't be where I am if I gave up. It is never too late to accomplish or achieve your goals. It doesn't matter your age, marital status, family size, color or background. All that matters is that you were able to do it. Don't give up; you may just be three feet from the gold.

Chapter 6

The Cause

A man who stands for nothing will fall for anything.

– Malcolm X

On 9/11/11, Diana Williams had an unforgettable experience. Williams and her husband were landlords for an apartment complex in New York City, and they were trying to evict tenants who hadn't paid their rent. Both Williams and her husband are hearing impaired. There was a controversy between the landlord and the tenants. The police were called. When the police arrived, they did not have an interpreter. Articles state that Chris, the husband, called the police using a video relay which should have signaled that a translator would be needed, but there was no translator when the cops arrived. Therefore, the cops could not understand Diana's side of the story. They could only go by the tenants' story because the tenants were not hearing impaired. Diana ended up arrested and detained for twenty four hours. During that time, Diana argued that her pleas for a sign language interpreter were ignored. Williams decided to fight for her rights. In the end, Diana received $750,000 for such a horrible ordeal. This case was the largest deaf discrimination settlement ever for an individual.

That is a perfect example of standing up for your rights and standing up for a cause. She paved a way for others to not back down from wrong treatment, especially when it involves the law. There are countless others who have stood their ground. With all the injustices in the world, there is much to stand up for these days. An individual shouldn't have to live in a country that does not enforce the law. Today's youth know very little, if any, about standing up for their rights.

No one knew this more than **Nelson Mandela**. He fought against apartheid in South Africa and spent twenty seven years in prison. Because of his stand, millions of people live a life of freedom. He then served as president of the same country where he was imprisoned.

Susan B. Anthony took a stand for equal rights for women to vote. She was arrested and convicted for illegally voting. She lobbied for the right for women to vote, and today she is considered as having a huge impact on the 19th Amendment which gives women the right to vote.

Sophie Scholl was a German student who was executed for treason. She took a stand and was resistant towards the Hitler and the Nazi party. She was an important symbol for German resistance. Many followed her brave stance.

Malala Yousafzai was a Pakistani schoolgirl who stood up for the right for girls to receive an education, defying the threats of Taliban. She was shot in the head for her stance. She survived and now more girls in her country will have the right to education.

Now, your stance may not be as serious as the ones mentioned above; however, there is always something to stand for. Not everyone will put their lives in harm's way or rally or start campaigns, but everyone should feel obligated in making sure justice is served individually and/or corporately. Whether you receive an unjust verdict, wrongful job termination, get pulled over by the cops because of the color of your skin or overcharged by a salesman, you must recognize that as a wrongdoing. Whether it is group discrimination where people are taking advantage of the elderly or children are being neglected or mistreated because of their handicaps, justice must be pursued and not ignored.

There are 3 things you need to know in order to stand up for a cause:

1. **Know your rights.** I know it may sound simple, but many people lose out because they are simply ignorant of what their rights are. You have to know what you are fighting for. We should know our rights as law abiding citizens, customers, entrepreneurs, employees, and students. What are your rights on the job? You should be compensated for over time. You shouldn't experience any type of harassment. What are your rights as tenants? What are your rights when you are rushed to the emergency room? There are rights to everything.

2. **Do your research.** Make sure you understand what you are up against. Understand the pros and cons, if any. Find out information about the statistics. Is this a world-wide issue? What are others saying about the injustice? I remember a story about one social activist who came against human trafficking. Before forming an

organization, she had to first research the areas in her community where human trafficking was prevalent. Then she had a target. Then she had to understand how it worked and what entities were connected with it. There was a process to the madness, and if she could get to the root causes and the beginning stages, she could be involved in prevention. Once she watched documentaries and interviewed police officers and victims, she had a better grasp of the epidemic and was able to form a very effective organization and get others involved.

3. **Stand.** Now it is time to take action. Action comes in different forms. Some forms are long term, and others are short term. It is best to use your gift or area of expertise. For example, with the different shootings pertaining to blacks and cops, many people have chosen to speak out against it in different ways. There are those looking to make an impact through law. Others through education, entertainment, family, and entrepreneurship.

Now, it is time to take the challenge. I challenge you to raise awareness of a social injustice in your community or if you feel that you have been wronged, stand up and fight for yourself. Your life and the lives of others depend on it. If you are an artist, draw a picture that depicts the truth. If you are a teacher, educate your students on social issues. If you are a singer, create a song that brings awareness to an issue. If you are a lawyer, fight the injustices. If you are a writer, write a book that depicts your personal story concerning a matter. By all means, if you are a human being, don't just stand by and watch injustice prevail if it is in your means to make a difference in your life and in the lives of others.

Chapter 7

Looking On the Bright Side: Creativity

**Creativity involves breaking out of established patterns in order to look at things in a different way. –
Edward de Bono**

Creativity is often birthed in hard times or when there is a problem to be solved. It is seen as a gift. Many people view going through obstacles as a negative experience, but it has a positive side or shall I say brighter side to it. I believe that brighter side overshadows the negativity once people understand that they can use obstacles to push them further. You discover things about yourself that you never would have if you weren't being pressed. Not only do you develop strength, but you begin to try to find a solution. In the midst of the process, great ideas are birthed. Creativity is a key factor to success.

According to Robert J. Szcxerba in the *4 Technologies Disrupting the Hearing Loss Industry article,* there are such great inventions as the MotionSavvy UNI which is a communication software that translates American Sign Language into speech and speech into text using a special camera that tracks the location of both hands and all ten fingers. Then there is the Solar Ear which is a solar powered battery that lasts for two to three years instead of the one week traditional battery usage span.

ISEEWHATYOUSAY captures spoken language on a smartphone and converts it into text and sends the text via Bluetooth to a remote user's device. Last but not least, there is my favorite, Hayleigh's Cherished Charms. Hayleigh was a ten year old girl who noticed that her classmates with hearing aids were hiding them behind their hair. Therefore, she wanted to make them feel proud and unashamed of their aids so she created fancy and shiny jewelry that could be classified as "hearing aid bling".

That's why creative thinking creates another platform and avenue to survive in this world. There are all kinds of people in this world who evolve using creative thinking. Operating in creativity does not just happen. It is a cognitive process that produces new ideas that transform old ideas into updated concepts. The preparation step of the creative process is when an individual becomes curious after encountering a problem. The world is full gravity! As we all see the world as a whole, we have to go out to conquer the world and to prove them wrong. There is greatness in all of us. Do not give up hope; keep faith in everything you do. As we should know life is never easy. We will always run into obstacles every day. Those obstacles can be used to create ingenious ideas.

What make us all unique when we face obstacles? Every person is unique. Every person is special, with unique combinations of abilities and needs that promotes ways to become successful. All of us deserve the opportunity and chance to learn in ways to make the most of our strengths and help us overcome our weaknesses. Use your uniqueness to create.

I had to explore new things. I used my creativity by starting my brand that will help the hearing and deaf culture. The ideas that I created will bring awareness and encouragement to our youth, the next generation. This brand will motivate them. I created a brand of back packs based upon an experience my son had. One day I picked him up from school. He was like mom I need another backpack because this one has a hole in it. But the hole was so small that you could barely see it. So I told him that I would buy another one. A few weeks went by, and he was still asking me for another backpack. I went ahead and purchased the back pack, and I gave it to him as a Christmas gift. Out all of his gifts that he received, he was really excited that he had a new backpack. All that mattered to me was seeing his face light up and the joy he had displayed. He just wanted something to carry his school supplies in. He gave me idea of how to be creative. The light bulb went off, and I created an awesome product based on his experience. You have to learn how to see things from a different perspective. Even children and adults tend to think and do things differently. It's all about trying to understand on their level. Either you have the skills or you don't. You have to train your thoughts and put forth practice. It's based on your mentality.

Special Chapter

For the Parents: Raising Hearing Impaired Kids

I raise my son to be himself, to never back down on things. If he feel like he can't do it, I encourage him to give it a try.

I wanted to take the time to help and inspire parents of hearing impaired or other disabled children suffering from autism, mental health, speech disorders, memory loss, etc. After all, parents are their child's first teacher and cheerleader. As mentioned earlier, I have a son that is hearing impaired, and it has not been easy. But I have an advantage because I understand and have lived through what he is going through. It has been challenging, but there are solutions.

Since it is family genetics, I wanted to make sure that my son had gotten his hearing test every year. From ages one to five, he passed the test. But, at any time it could relapse in the future. My son attended Pre-K and Kindergarten back in my home town, and he was doing just fine. One day his Kindergarten teacher noticed something about him. He would not reply back to her or follow directions in class. Both she and the office staff were aware of our family history. So they gave him hearing test at the school, and he failed it. I couldn't believe it because he had just taken and passed a hearing test. But deep inside I knew it was time for another test from his audiologist. I knew the school audiology test was not adequate enough because it takes more than just having a kid to raise his hands to each beep sound to check for hearing. So I took him back to his audiologist who specializes in this area so that he could be fully tested, and they could determine the loss by the nerves. Well he passed it again, and I informed the school and supplied the proper paperwork. It didn't mean he was 100% okay. His teacher, speech and audiology staff still knew to keep a close eye on him, and I was grateful for that. His first two years with school had been amazing, and all his teachers loved him. He passed to the first grade. He received speech therapy for two years there. They did a great job in providing proper accommodation.

While he was finished his year in Kindergarten, we were in the process of moving to another state. So, it was time for another hearing test at age five. He failed it with a slight mild hearing loss, which is not bad, so we got him hearing aids. I wasn't worried because I knew how to handle this because I had gone through it myself. It was like a reflection of my process. I was able to stay strong for him and made sure he was on track and ahead. During that summer, I moved to another state. I was concerned about my son having to attend another school because in our new location the academic programs operate under a faster pace. They started school later at age level, which meant you had to be 4 years old by September 1st to start Pre -K which is different from my home town because you had to be 4 years old before September 30th. Thank God, my son finished his last two years at his old school.

I was a little curious about him making that transition from one state to another because of the language and age level of other kids starting school. I was looking for a school for him to attend. So my uncle and aunt happened to find one for him in their school zone. I went by the school to secure a spot, and I spoke with the principal about his situation. She was in awe because I could tell that she was not prepared for that. She told me not to worry because he is in good hands. I kind of felt relief, but at the same time, I did my part to make sure that the school was doing what they needed to do.

During his first grade year, due to his hearing loss, I made sure that all of his teachers, the principal, speech, and office staff were fully aware of what was going on. His teacher and the principal were by far the worst. As soon as school started, it was time for Assessment/Dars/IEP meeting for him. They also did a hearing test on him which I already told them from start that he has hearing loss. They kept trying to label him and find every excuse as to why his reading comprehension was much lower than the other students. I'd already told them that his hearing loss played a part in that.

I'd never seen my child so discouraged. Every meeting I had with his teacher, she was in a rush. That let me know that she didn't have time to work or want to put forth the effort to make sure he had the proper classroom accommodations. They even did some damn psychology study to see why his behavior was the way it was. They studied his facial expressions, hand movements, and verbiage. I told them that that was normal for a kid with hearing loss, so don't try to study my damn child like he's your lab study. He was acting his age.

Every time it was time for an evaluation meeting, all I would hear is this or that. I wanted to hear what they had planned on doing to help accommodate myself and supply a learning environment for him. It was if no one at the school had any experience dealing with this type of situation. The whole school year had been a disaster, and there were no proper accommodation or resources. The school should have been prepared for this kind of situation for any students with any type of disability no matter what. Any child has a right to attend a public school, and it is a law to have arrangements ready in advance. He was promoted to the second grade, even though he was below reading level. There were documents from his audiologist, and that is why they were able to waive it and move him up.

His second grade teacher was better, but the school was still was in the process of trying to figure out what would be the right way to assist my child. It was frustrating because his teacher still was oblivious to certain aspects of his hearing loss. His teacher really upset me one day. She told me that when all the students sit on the floor, G'Ivori doesn't pay attention because he moves and plays around. She made it seems as if he has a behavior problem. That is what six year olds do, and you can't forget that he has a hearing loss. I know my child, and as a mother I should. I had been going up to his school up to three times a week during those two years to make sure they were doing their job correctly. A parent should not have to go through that.

He was retained in second grade because he was below reading level. I understood that.

As mothers, parents or guardians, we have to do what is right and protect our kids. I removed my son from that school, and he attended second grade at another school which was in my school zone. I'd heard so many great things about that school and how they accommodate their students. So I went and enrolled him at the new school. I spoke with the principal and staff. She assured me that they already had a program in place. I felt as if a burden was lifted off of my shoulders. The school counselors also had experience in working with deaf and hearing impaired students. And to this point, I'm glad I made the right decision in sending him there. My son has shown progress and has had the best teachers and staff whom knew how to work with him. He was happy and loved it there. Ever since he had attended this new school, I hadn't had to go up to the school to check on him. I did what was best for my child.

Raising a partial deaf and/or deaf child requires three main factors:

Patience

Love

Teaching

Patience is a virtue. When raising children, patience is a key regardless. But with hearing impaired youth, more patience is needed. They learn differently so things have to be broken down in different ways. They may learn slower than others. You may have to spend extra time with them on homework. You have to communicate with them in a different way.

Love is a key factor. Deaf children sometimes feel left out and need the extra attention. They feel isolated because they are being treated differently than the other kids and aren't able to catch on as quickly as others. Your love will be a reinforcement of their confidence.

Teaching. Teaching them to stand up for themselves is vital. Pay attention to your child's comments about school and the way others are treating them. Teach them about their rights and having a voice. Teach them to be bold but respectful and to not accept anything less than the best. Of course they will have to learn on their own, but you as a parent have to be conscious of that process and help guide them to the best of their ability.

Once you stumble upon obstacles, do not let them bring you down. Keep fighting and continue to find your way. Your children's childhood depends on it.

"My vulnerability is my greatest disability."

Leola Smith

Source Notes

1. America, Hearing Loss Association of. "Basic Facts About Hearing Loss | Hearing Loss Association of America." *HLAA Updates.* N.p., n.d. Web. 2 Oct. 2016.

2. Mathias, Christopher. "Deaf Woman to Get $750,000 for Hellish Ordeal with NYPD." *Huffington Post.* HuffingtonPost.com, Inc., 28 Oct. 2015. Web. 2 Oct. 2016.

3. Szczerba, Robert J. "4 Technologies Disrupting the Hearing Loss Industry." *The Next Web.* N.p., 20 July 2015. Web. 10 Oct. 2016.

4. Sugar, Meredith. "Response to Washington Post Article about Nyle DiMarco." *Response to Washington Post Article about Nyle DiMarco | AG Bell | Listening and Spoken Language.* Alexander Graham Bell Association for the Deaf and Hard of Hearing, n.d. Web. 02 July 2017.

www.ingramcontent.com/pod-product-compliance
Lightning Source LLC
Chambersburg PA
CBHW071750090426
42738CB00011B/2621